M–80

Also by Jim Daniels

Poetry

Places/Everyone, 1985
Punching Out, 1990

Chapbooks

Factory Poems, 1979
On the Line, 1981
The Long Ball, 1988
Digger's Territory, 1989
Hacking It, 1992

M-80

224

Jim Daniels

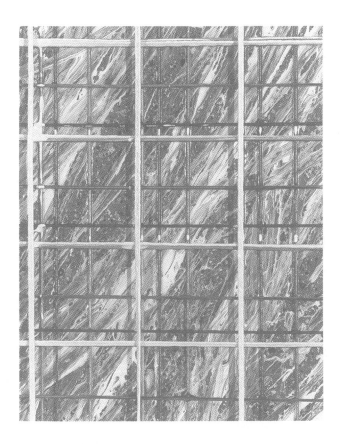

University of Pittsburgh Press
Pittsburgh • London

The publication of this book is supported by grants from the National Endowment for the Arts in Washington, D.C., a Federal agency, and the Pennsylvania Council on the Arts.

Published by the University of Pittsburgh Press, Pittsburgh, Pa. 15260

Library of Congress Cataloging-in-Publication Data

Daniels, Jim, 1954-
    M–80 / Jim Daniels.
        p.   cm.—(Pitt poetry series)
    ISBN 0-8229-3747-6 (hard : alk. paper). —ISBN 0-8229-5497-4 (pbk. : alk. paper)
    I. Title. II Title: M-eighty. III. Series.
    PS3554.A5635M15   1993   92-62335
    811'.54—dc20   CIP

A CIP catalogue record for this book is available from the British Library.

The author and publisher wish to express their grateful acknowledgment to the following publications in which some of these poems first appeared: *Bassettown Review* ("Orange Driver"); *The Bellingham Review* ("Fire"); *Burning World* ("Digger, Deep Snow," "Digger Takes His Dog for a Walk," "Digger, the Birthday Boy," "Digger Ties One On"); *Colorado Review* ("Broke," "Still Lives: Sweat," formerly "Still Lives in Detroit, #11"); *Gargoyle* ("Digger's Territory"); *The Journal* ("In Black Gloves," "Raw October"); *Light Year 88–89* ("Detroit Hymns, Christmas Eve"); *The MacGuffin* ("Anthem"); *Michigan Quarterly Review* ("Joy Ride," "M-80," "Still Lives: Benitau Street"); *Mid-American Review* ("Digger's Trip"); *North Dakota Quarterly* ("Parked Car"); *Ohio Review* ("On the Other End"); *The Pennsylvania Review* ("Wild Country"); *The Pittsburgh Quarterly* ("Universal City"); *Planet Detroit* ("Digger Goes to Church"); *Poetry East* ("Digger Pays Off the Mortgage," "How Much Light"); *Red Brick Review* ("1977"); *River Styx* ("Passing"); *Tabula Rasa* ("Crazy Eddie"); *West Branch* ("One of Those Things") and *Witness* ("Trouble at the Drive-In").

Some of these poems also appeared in the chapbooks *Digger's Territory* (Adastra Press) and *Hacking It* (Ridgeway Press).

Paperback cover painting by Darryl Stawinski, "15"
Book design by Frank Lehner

Contents

4. Trouble at the Drive-In

1

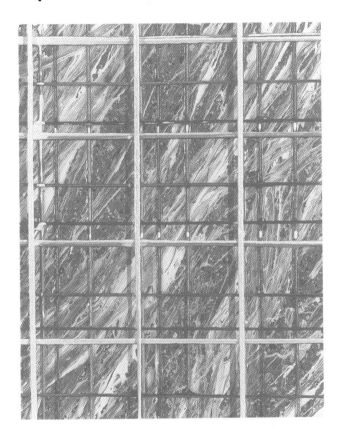

Wild Country

WILD COUNTRY

Behind the Northeast Trucking garage
in a field of oil-stained weeds, rusty parts,
I sat next to the bottle-breaking rock.

I picked up a piece of green glass
and held it to the light, flooding cool sadness
over the broken-down trucks in the fenced-in yard.

The guard dog barked its viciousness
against the fence, punctuating the memory
of my father's blows.

Dinner churned in my stomach.
A rat crawled through the high, coarse weeds.
I pulled my jacket tight, zipped it up.

I'd ducked a clumsy slap and run here.
It was one more than I thought I deserved.
My face still burned.

I tried to spit out the faint taste
of blood. Twisted limbs of bare trees
faded into sky.

High-school kids would show up soon
to smoke pot and drink cheap wine.
I sat till I heard feet

crunching broken glass
and my father's voice calling my name
like he was lost, a little lost.

M-80

ROBERT KENNEDY SHOT. Early June
my mother prayed the rosary
in front of the hollow crucifix in her room
that slid open to reveal death candles
hidden for last rites' blessing.
They'd get used soon enough.

She prayed a long time. My father
wanted dinner. We ate mac-and-cheese.
Wipe your mouth
you've got that orange stuff all over it.
You're a big boy now—try to eat right.
A day when everything stuck to my face,
my 12th birthday. *Postponed,*
my mother whispered through tears.

▼

Bobby. Bobby Kennedy, Debbie said,
balancing on the curb. She wore
a white blouse, shirttail out over cutoffs.
She drew a blue heart on her tennis shoe.
I wanted to fill it in.

What could we do
in the gray light of clouds
and broken glass, the stale wads
of gum clutching against our teeth?
It was after a rain and we rode through puddles
it was a banana-seat stingray
it was one speed and one speed only.
She rode behind me on the seat
her thin legs swaying just above the ground.

We bought Twinkies and Orange Crushes
at the store. I said *I have an orange crush
on you.* She laughed. The sun was going down
somewhere.

My birthday got rained out, I told her.
Assassinated. Our laughs short,
hollow. *Why does everybody
hate everybody?* Debbie asked.
Her parents had just split.
I don't hate you, I said.

Look at you, she said and put down
her Crush, licked the cream around my lips.
An M-80 went off in my chest—at least
it seemed that way. I'd bought five of them
from Artie Pilkowski, saving them for the 4th.
But I would use one soon enough
to blow up a mailbox—I was not immune.
Artie lost part of his hand that summer,
another of those hard-way lessons
we kept hearing about.

▼

Behind the store we held each other and kissed
birthday kisses even after it was dark
even after it rained some more.

I kicked up my kickstand and rode her home
under the blue streetlights. She held on
tighter than I've ever been held.
My brother stood on the corner

smoking with his friends.
Junior's got a girlfriend, they chanted.
We were fierce and serious as I pedaled past.

My mother was praying again, and the TV was off.
I knelt beside her, my elbows sinking
into the soft bed, offering up my small explosions.

Crazy Eddie

wasn't crazy. He was a drunk garbageman
with a bad temper.

He shot Porters' pigeons
for shitting on his garage.
The Porters who had no kids
and gave us each a sucker
if we stood on their porch and sang
their name: *Porter, Porter-er*
like good little boys.

They dressed their dog Pee Wee
in tiny sweaters, gave him his own room.
They built a high stone wall
between their house and Eddie's.

He took our balls
when they landed in his yard.
A whole box of them we saw
through a basement window.

▼

In his bright white T-shirt
and green work pants,
in his greased-back hair
and beer gut, thick forearms
and squint and scowl,
he drenched his lawn in toxic fertilizers.
His two daughters played alone
on the sidewalk.

He set fire to the field
behind his house where we played ball.
Crazy, Crazy Eddie we shouted, running

past his house, midnight.
Devil's Night he hid in the bushes
with a pellet gun. His cigarette glowed.

We didn't know then
he picked up trash for a living
and drank twelve beers a night.
Maybe all he wanted was a green lawn
and a peaceful drunk.

▼

Years later, I worked in the beer store
where every day he brought his empties.
He said hello to me then,
and thank you. I handed him
his change, looked him in the eye.
I am the one who burned *fuck you*
into his lawn.

Maybe we just weren't smart enough then
to know who to hate, a bucketful of balls
the only wealth we understood.
Hauling garbage all day, the stink
and mess of it. A perfect lawn.
What did we know, just a bunch of kids
learning that you had to sing,
sing for your candy.

UNIVERSAL CITY

It was enough of a thrill
to ride the bus down Dequindre to Universal City
our first indoor mall, to drool over posters
of naked women at Spencer's Gifts
pointing and laughing till we got kicked out,
even Sonny who told his mother what CMF meant
so we had to change the name of our bowling team.

It was enough of a thrill to eat burgers
at the Red Barn across from the mall
much less have some guy pull a gun.
We ducked but he didn't shoot.
His girlfriend and another guy
eating hamburgers together.

The guy with the gun swore and cried
as the cops carried him away.
We were so high on that danger,
when Fred tried to spit and it landed
on his pants, we didn't even laugh.

▼

No matter what we thought
we were not Crazy Mother Fuckers—
we'd only recently explained to Larry
what you did to make babies.
He said *My mom and dad don't fuck*
and ran away. Who could blame him then
for not being able to imagine it,
his father a short bald accountant
older than all our fathers, his mother
too shy to answer the door.

Universal City, Red Barn, breaking up
the soft Jell-O of another summer day.
Soon enough we'd be puking on the sides of cars
and trying to force ourselves
on any girl we could get within arm's reach.
Soon enough we'd fall in love hard enough
to embarrass ourselves in public places.

It wasn't the last time we'd see a gun.
Four years later, Fred's brother
stole a car, shot some guy, gave him
a last beer, then finished him off.

Those summer days moved slow and thick
as hot tar. We wanted anything
that'd speed them up. But even then
the underground streams were flowing,
gurgling to the surface
in remote spots. Universal City
seemed light years away then,
and a man with a gun crying over a woman
was a man from another planet,
a faint speck in the distant sky.

FIRE

We joined altar boys
to hold matches in our hands,
to light the wax taper, reach up
to light wicks we couldn't see—
only the quiet flame popping up success.

The Holy Week incense spun
through the solemn church.
One hissing match sparked
what we thought death might smell like.

▼

We bought silver lighters
fluid and flints to light
cigarettes, ants, and spiders—
to flick open and shut
through hot summer days.
Behind Northeast Trucking we set
the field on fire, put it out,
set it on fire, put it out,
each time letting it spread further
through dry weeds.

▼

When Judy's house burned
a fireman wrapped her in a blanket
on the front lawn, trying
to squeeze her back
as we watched from the street.

If you don't know the smell
there is nothing I can tell you.
If you know the smell
there is nothing I can tell you.

In black gloves

and jean jackets, we met
on late October nights cold enough
to crack in two. *Not cold,*
not cold I yelled back at my mother,
stepping out, my ears already numb.

Cigarette smoke rose with our breath
behind the bowling alley as we imagined
fast cars and girls with rat-tail combs.
We felt tough as our older brothers,
stepping into bright stores to steal
what fit under our thin jackets, dragging
our pointed boots, horseshoe cleats sparking.

On those nights I learned
to say *fuck* with authority, to slice open
the cold with my little blade.
Kick ass, kick ass we spat, but stuck
to our own turf, slap-boxing, turning
our collars up against what we didn't know.

A coldness lay thick in my throat
walking home alone on those clear nights
late again, clenching and unclenching
those black gloves as if I held the night
in my own hands.

RAW OCTOBER

We toss eggs
at cars, houses,
Crazy Eddie chases
us down the street
Larry rips
his shirt on a fence
Fred loses a shoe
through the backyards
we outrun
yapping dogs, get away
clean to smoke cigarettes
behind Northeast Trucking.

We pry off hubcaps
fling them toward
the puffy white moon
they clatter and roll
echo up and down
the street.

Why do we do this?
Somebody should catch us
and smack us around a little.
Eventually they do.

PASSING

In gym class boxing, Fat Feeney got paired
with Big Eddie Lavendar. Coach Wendler
circled the ring, taunted Feeney,
pushed him back when he tried to run.

Lavendar flattened Feeney's nose.
He wouldn't get up. Lay there frozen,
an iceberg waiting for arctic silence.
We filed past to the locker room
kicking him, spitting out all our names
for boys like him who wouldn't fight.

The High Dive: *A* for a dive. *C* for a jump.
F for sissies. Feeney climbed up, jiggling
layers of flesh. We wanted to see the splash.
Coach screamed *Jump Feeney jump!*
We chanted *Jump Feeney jump!*
Our voices echoed off tile, rang out
over still water. Feeney held the rail.
His tears fell to the board. We waited, screaming,
bare-assed on the benches.
When he climbed down, Wendler paddled him.
In the locker room, our arms popped out,
punched him between the rows.

Doug Molinski stomped on Feeney's face
in the parking lot. Everyone knew
he never fought back, a punching bag
for anyone's random black-and-blue anger.
Molinski wouldn't stop because,

because, who knows. Feeney's face
a bloody mess surgery couldn't fix.

Coach used to yell
You're a big boy, Feeney,
hit somebody, as if those two things
went hand in hand. Molinski back in a year.
Feeney's mother took him away—who knows where.

You know how dogs can sniff out fear?
Yeah, I punched him a few times:
jab, jab, jab. I took my *C*.

ORANGE DRIVER

Tonight you see Molinski
outside Lenny's Party Store
and think *what the hell*

and call to him
and give him your money
and he buys for you, Orange Driver.

You're not sure
what's in the stuff. The main thing:
it's strong.

He doesn't give you
any change but you say nothing
because he is big and strong

and the main thing is: he's mean.
He asks you where the party is
because it's a Friday night

and there's always a party.
You tell him you don't know.
He is hanging over your window

and your heart's beating fast enough
to make you guzzle the bottle a little quicker
once he leaves. You do know

where the party is, at Lisa Something's
over on Alvina, but he's Molinski,
Mr. Bad News. You don't know the address

but you'll look for cars. It's raining
and already lights blur the wet street
which means a basement party

not a backyard party which means
somebody at the door might not let you in.
But everybody gets in tonight

including Molinski, who shows up
late and drunker than you are
and when he sees you, you look away

but he has seen you. He comes over and gives you
a little shove. *Hey buddy, are you*
fucked up yet? And you say, *Yeah man,*

I'm fucked up, and smile, but he's got
the mean hard look. You back away a little.
He closes in—another shove.

I thought you didn't know
where the party was and you start to say
something but he pops you in the mouth.

You hold your mouth and try to turn
your back toward him, but he's not through:
Are you fucked up yet? A punch

in the eye. *Are you fucked up yet?*
No one has stood between you and him.
You want someone to stand there. Anyone

to block his clear path. You start
shoving your way up the stairs and out the door
toward the gate, swallowing blood

but there's too much ground
too much wet ground between you and your car.
He grabs your back, knees you

in the kidneys, you fall, your stomach
erupting vomit onto the slick grass.
It is what will save you—

yeah, he's fucked up
you hear him say, quieter.
Still, no one stands between him and you.

The others watch silently.
Everyone's heard about Feeney's face,
the plastic surgery and why he moved.

You are puking, so he walks away.
You are puking and can only see out one eye.
Puke and blood. Orange Driver.

You're soaked from the grass. Some people
help you to your feet. Lisa Something
thanks you for not telling where the party was.

Somebody told though.
Somebody's called the police—
you hear the helicopter's spinning blades.

Their searchlights run the streets,
settle in on Lisa's house.
Two cop cars pull up as you slink away.

The street's clogged with cars leaving,
cops yelling, a mess of lights and noise.
You just want clear pavement, darkness, silence.

You are sick everywhere. The rain,
tiny bullets bouncing off your hood.
Maybe he won't remember, you are thinking

but you know he will remember. And the main thing is:
he's mean. You sit in the street in front
of your house, spitting blood, working on a story,

a good story, to tell your parents. Or else
the truth, or enough of the truth to get change back
from what you'll surely have to pay.

PARKED CAR

Fred and I, drunk and stoned,
drove around laughing like we did
in the old days before I met Karen.
Then I said *drive by Karen's*
and he said *are you sure?*
Then he said *okay* like he was tired
and didn't want to end up
bailing me out again.
She'd given my ring back a month ago.
I knew she had a date.

A car was parked where I always parked.
Fred pulled in on the other side of the street.
We sat there. *There's no one in the car*
Fred said. *No one in the car.*
No lights in the house. I squinted hard
through the dark, saw a head
pop up above the seat then down again.
I reached for the door.
There's no one in the car—
we're leaving now, Fred said.
He put his hand on my shoulder
gentle, firm.

▼

I turned to stone then crumbled
wanting her and not wanting her
while Fred drove me home.
I held my open hand out the window
against the cold wind.

Twelve years ago.
Today in a moment rain
changes to snow.
Maybe it was Fred I loved that night.
We'd have never called it that.
And I still wouldn't to his face—
that small touch
during the years when none of us
ever touched each other.

Sometimes I still drive by that spot
with my wife, who doesn't know the ghosts
living there. We don't kiss in cars anymore.
Karen married, moved away.

Ah, heart. Hearts.
Mine and yours. Yeah, all of you.
The times we've given it away
for chump change.
The heart, the fist. If you're lucky
someone grabs your shoulder.

DETROIT HYMNS, CHRISTMAS EVE

Kenny and I down a few beers
circling church in my old Falcon
thinking about midnight mass.

White Castle is the closest we get,
sitting at the shiny metal counter
mumbling our little prayers.
Shoulda got a pint of something,
Kenny says.

Shoulda woulda coulda mouda.
It's a bum wearing three hats,
the high priest. He winks at us, falls asleep.

Let's not argue about drinking.
A young couple slide off their stools,
bump heads going out the door.

Ratburger, I say, chomping down
on one of the four I ordered.
Ratboogers, Kenny says.

Rats ain't got no boogers.
It's the plump woman behind the counter,
safe in her hair net.

Kenny punches the jukebox:
Mitch Ryder's "Little Latin Lupe Lu,"
and a couple old Motown.

Let's dance, Sugar, Kenny says.
The counter woman shakes her hips a little

but she clearly don't got the spirit:
What's that mean, Latin Loop De Lou?

It's a Christmas song, Kenny says.
The grill man with bad skin
laughs at that—his spit sizzles.

ANTHEM

Two months after retirement
my father is here, to get away
from 6 A.M. and his cup
of empty destination.

At a football game we huddle
under his umbrella
talking about the obvious.
He brings me coffee
to hold warm between my hands,
a gift of no occasion.

When we rise for the anthem
I hear the rusty crack of his voice
for the first time maybe ever.

Thirty-three years of coughing
thick factory air, of drifting to sleep
through the heavy ring of machinery,
of twelve-hour days. In my sleep
I felt the cold bump of his late-night kiss.

I shiver in the rain
as my father sings me
what now I hear as
a children's song. I lean into him,
the umbrella and rain my excuse,
my shoulder against his,
and I imagine my mother
falling in love.

2

Time, Temperature

TIME, TEMPERATURE

—for James Baldwin

1967, Detroit. My grandfather watches
tracer bullets zing past
his window. The National Guard's taken over
Lillibridge School on the corner.

    He remembers the strike at Packard
    when they promoted blacks,
    then the riots in '43,
    how the crowds gathered on Belle Isle
    just down the road, all the bloodshed
    just down the road.

On the phone with my father, he is saying *niggers*
and my father is saying *Dad* he is saying
Dad stay in the house, stay away from the window.

    My grandfather has his theories
    why they can't take the cold
    can't skate can't swim
    why they can't park their cars
    why grape's their favorite flavor
    why if you get bit by one with purple lips
    it will kill you.

My father shakes his head into thick air
saying *stay away, stay away.*
A drop of sweat hits the dirty kitchen floor.
Dad. Dad. My father's long sigh.

▼

Eenie, meanie miney moe
catch a nigger by the toe

our toes wedged in a tight circle
to see who'd be It. My mother
wouldn't let us say *nigger*.
She said say *froggy*.
We said *froggy*. The other kids said
froggy?

She washed my mouth with soap.
Where did you hear that word?
Everywhere. *Where?*

▼

1967. Eleven, I climbed on the garage
with my father's camera. In the streaked photos
flocks of helicopters blotch the sky, nothing
like birds. I held on to the rough shingles
as the spinning blades roared above me.
Helicopters spilled guardsmen
onto the armory lawn on Eight Mile Road,
the border between Detroit and Warren.

We lived on that edge. Sirens
wailed their crazy tune, no Motown Sound,
nothing we could dance to.

Fear of heights seemed more real
than what I heard on the radio, than rumors
panting on the street: *They're at Belmont.*
They're at Farwell Field.
They're crossing Eight Mile.

Getting up was easy. I needed help
getting down, my feet dangling in air,
the camera somersaulting down onto the grass.

▼

Eight Mile Road. Six lanes wide. The long barbed
shout, pale slab, sizzling fuse.

I didn't know a black person till I was nineteen.
I could have almost shouted from my porch.

▼

Nigger pile. Riding nigger.
Nigger pile on Tony. Nigger beard.
Nigger stompers. Nigger-rigged.
Nigger-lipped. Niggered up. Nigger toes.
Nigger Heaven. How far
you have to chase that nigger
to get that shirt? A fight, a fight
a nigger and a white.

Should I explain the terms, include an index
and glossary? Do we all possess
such footnotes, filed, hidden, backwards,
in code, watermarks revealed by light?

Plenty of words for hate around here.
Like Eskimos with snow, we have
our subtle distinctions.

No one can trace
all the secret white tunnels
or break the white code.
Invisible, white on white.
Squint and hope for the best.

▼

1970. Roger Edwards, our new history teacher,
gave us roles to play: KKK members,
Black Panthers. I was Huey Newton.
I said *honky* and *pig* a lot.
I wore a black beret. We dressed in black,
took toy guns to class.

I learned a little about the burning fuse—
Bobby Seale, H. Rap Brown, Stokeley Carmichael.
If this town don't come around . . .

We knew our town hadn't, and how it burned.
Huey Newton walking into our class
would have turned us all to tin soldiers,
turned us all to brittle glass.

Roger taught us what he could
till the nuns fired him.
He played records by Lightning Hopkins,
Coltrane, such strangeness we wanted to like
because he liked it. He let us swear in class
but he made us swear
not to say *nigger.*

▼

Our fathers worked with their fathers
in factories in Detroit and Warren,
brought their hate home in greasy lunch pails:
better watch out for that nigger.
That's a nigger department.
Don't help that nigger,
lazy nigger.

It spilled across the dinner tables,

through the muddy alleys,
across the concrete playgrounds,
into the schools, and we learned
our lessons well.

▼

1974. Black students
from Pershing High two miles away
visited Fitzgerald, my school.
We asked them questions
in a room crowded with teachers
who prompted us in whispers.
So foreign even those translators couldn't help.
Stilted as a high-school play.
Someone took pictures for the yearbook.

They filled our halls with a flavor
foreign and pungent. Some new kind of cooking
I wasn't sure about.
The next day in class we sat glum
while a perky teacher preached brotherhood.
We knew better. *They only brought*
the nice ones, somebody said.

▼

1975. I worked in a liquor store
where we didn't cash checks for blacks
but sold them booze and cigarettes.

A man held a gun to my head
where's your hiding place
where's your fuckin' hiding place?
I said we don't have a hiding place

he said *motherfucker, everybody
got a hiding place*
I said we took it to the bank
he said *I'm gonna kill you motherfucker
where's your hiding place?*

We stood there, his gun brushing my temple.
We looked each other in the eye: no recognition.
He grabbed money from the register,
took off down Eight Mile. I reached down
and fingered the cigarette carton
filled with checks and twenties.
The boss called the cops.
Fingerprints on a can of Colt .45
and no clues or suspects.
Colt .45, I said, *figures.*

I flipped through the mug shots:
some nigger, I said.

▼

Carl the gun collector
handed out rifles to the neighbors
in '67: *just in case just in case
they cross Eight Mile. To protect
our families and homes,* he said.
The right to bear arms.
My father did not take one.

In 1974 under the threat of busing
neighbors took pledges
put signs in their windows
I will not send my kids.

I will keep my kids home.
My mother took no sign.

The Supreme Court ruled against
cross-district busing.
Neighbors smiled archly
no thanks to you, as if my mother
was a scab in this union town.

My grandparents both got mugged
on their street. My grandmother bent
into a sad old turtle in her chair
dazed and afraid, black circles
deep under her eyes in the house
her parents built.

We ate early when they came over
so they could be home before dark.
The golden rule: home before dark.

My grandfather would not move,
spraying his hose on the fire
in the abandoned house next door,
buying up the vacant lots around him
ten bucks a piece.

They watched their one good television
in a living room lined with three broken ones
so they won't know which one to take.

9000 vacant lots in their old neighborhood,
another 1000 homes empty, boarded up.

There's only three things
wrong with blacks, my grandfather said.
They lie, they steal, and they kill.
He did say *blacks.*

▼

My grandfather loaded up his old Ford
with stale baked goods from Sanders,
bruised fruit and vegetables, to distribute
to the poor for Father Connors, the priest
from the church across the street.
St. Rose, razed now, just another vacant lot.

He fixed bikes for the black kids
on his street. Kids. Kids
were kids, the contradictions
rattling around his head,
as if he had separate brains
for theory and practice,
separate hearts.

Old man. All things harden inside him.
No way to explain generations
of prejudice, poverty, and hunger,
bad schools and no hope, and hate,
no way to explain it.

In Detroit, it has always been a matter
of taking sides. *They
drove us out of Detroit,* he says.

▼

My old neighborhood in Warren
redlined. Too close
to Eight Mile. Blacks moving in.
Property values plunging.
Shoulda sold years ago,
a realtor said.

Old neighbors move out, refining their excuses.
Two streets over, a black family lines the curb
with boulders to keep cars off their lawn.

▼

A black guy on the assembly line
offered to break my machine for me
accidentally. I nodded.
We stood together, not smiling
just breathing and waiting

waiting and resting
resting and sighing
sighing and nodding.

The nod. It's too easy
to say *That's the kind
of cooperation we need.*
That's the kind of cooperation we need.

▼

Dogs growl. Women peek out curtains.
A black man is delivering circulars
on a hot August afternoon in 1968

surrounded by the echo of his own steps.
He is coming up our walk.
My mother opens the door, offers him iced tea.
I sit on the stoop next to him
staring, a child staring.
My mother leans against the bricks.
I can hear his throat swallowing
the cold tea. Little
is said and what is said
is said about the heat.
Thank you, he says. *Back to work.*

Hope your mom washed that glass good.
Something I will hear from time
to time. Not too loud or
too mean, but I will hear it.

1980. In the department store,
those foam packing chips that last forever
poured from an overhead funnel
into gift boxes full of vases, clocks, books,
ceramic dogs, martini glasses, china, silver.
To cushion and protect.

Kim's dark skin
surrounded by the white, white foam.
We worked in that blizzard together.
We leaned across the table toward each other
in the basement under the store
where all the black people worked,
along with me and another white kid.

We felt like robots down there,
filling and sealing. Till our eyes locked
in the hard stare of mannequins.
We ate lunch together
in the lounge. People talked.
It only took me a year to ask her out.
Dixie scowled. *What are you doing?*
This is Detroit you're talking about.

We went to a movie in my part of town,
for coffee in her part.
I can't remember what we saw
because I held her hand in the dark
and we were alone there just like
two white kids, or two black kids.

All night the stares bit into us
like tiny bugs we couldn't see.
Walking to the car, I squeezed
her hand into a fist.
I guess you have to be rich
to get away with it, she said
and maybe she was right.

Our own sizzling skins could not
our own good fire could not blend
or overwhelm or distract or soothe enough.
We were not rich enough or fast enough, fat enough
or thick-and-thin enough. We could not slam
our car doors loud enough to break the long stare.

In her apartment, her child cried
upstairs while we held each other on the couch.

Go home white boy, somebody yelled
when I got in my car.

At work the next day
the foam rained down between us.
It lay in heaps.
I couldn't look at her.
I grabbed two handfuls and squeezed:
nothing can destroy them.

I said *some nigger robbed the store*
and the cop said *What else is new?*
Get a gun, he said.
The board tilts, and all the balls
roll into the same hole.

I felt bad, but I said it anyway.
My shrunken head, tiny eyes
sewn shut. There is no
immunization, no shot, no cure,
no pill, no magic, no saint,
no argument, no prophet,
no potion, no confession,
no gift, no miracle, no fucking miracle.

No.

Last summer, the dog next door
scared away two black kids
trying to break into my basement.

I saw them running away. A week later
the same two kids cased out a house
down the street. I stood at the door
watching, sweating, heart jumping.

I stepped out toward them. They said
You keep following us you're gonna get hurt.
I said *I'm only trying to protect my property.*
They said *Listen man, you wanna get hurt?*

No, I don't want to get hurt.
Yes, I have property now,
an old house in this mixed neighborhood.
Maybe I was afraid because they were black.
Maybe they were angry because I was white.
I tried to talk calmly but I know enough
about being stoned to know
they were stoned on something.
Everybody stoned on something—
stoned on history and hate.

Everybody got a hiding place.

▼

Pressed flat to the shingles
a little afraid of the height
as the helicopters pass
a little afraid of the noise and sirens
a little afraid of blacks
and rumors and everything I don't understand:
why burn, why here?

▼

1990. Waiting for the light at Eight Mile and I-75
I see a naked black man lunge between cars,
two cops chasing him, his feet slapping
hot cement in the silence of engines idling July heat
two cops chasing him down the road
between Detroit and Warren
between two hard places
and he is naked and soft and running
till the cops wrestle him to the ground
scraping his knees and chin.
I pass by as he lies there getting cuffed.
As he lies there.

He looks a little dazed. The cops lift him
by the cuffs and he stands, his arms
tight behind him. He looks a little stoned
a little stoned on something.
The cuffs cut into his wrists
but he barely flinches.
Even naked, he barely flinches.

Maybe his story is the story I want to tell.
But I do not know his story.

I do not know what he has done.
I am telling you everything I know.

▼

Carl took his guns back
but they are someplace.
Carl moved away
but he is someplace.

I know Carl. His nose twitches
with the gunpowder of his own hate.

They are someplace.

I am trying to be naive.
It has come down to this.
Naive enough to keep from being rolled
into another bitter pill.

An open fire hydrant in hot August
after an afternoon game at Tiger Stadium.
I am walking toward my car.
A young black kid, maybe six, is dancing
in his underwear in the cool spray
he is holding his wrists up toward the sky
as if to say *take me, take me like this*
and I am so hot I join him
dancing too in cutoffs and T-shirt

and I raise my arms above my head
thinking *yes, I would like to be taken like this*
and we dance under the same sun
and there is room enough for both of us
in the spray on Rosa Parks Boulevard
in Detroit in Michigan in America saying
take me take me under one big sun
that will take us, take us all
in its own good time.

3

Digger's Territory

DIGGER, THE BIRTHDAY BOY

Forty years old. Twenty at the plant.
When you started, you said
two years tops. Enough money
to get ahead a little
till I figure out what I
really want to do.
When someone calls you a lifer now
you do not object.

Your buddy Frank took an early
retirement buy out, moved down south
near his parents. He sent a picture—
it's on the bulletin board—he's holding
his belly like a watermelon:
I'm going crazy
down here. Heard any good jokes?
Thirty years. And out.

He got an aerial view of the plant
that everyone signed—the company gift.
Roof and parking lot. He squinted,
shook his head, forced a laugh,
like it was a bachelor party, everybody
trying hard to be funny, drinking fast.
And him a lifetime bachelor.

You don't see the guys after work
anymore. No quick showers
to head out to the bars, hair wet
and shiny, the night fresh with possibility.
No card games, ball games, picnics. Just talk
at breaks about cars, sports, TV, family.

Family. You sit in the car after work today
wondering what you'll get when you get home—
a card from the kids, your favorite meal,
burgers on the grill, cake and ice cream.
You back your car out and smile,
swerving onto Mound Road toward home,
toward the off-key voices,
the new shirt, socks, shovel.

DIGGER TIES ONE ON

Foreman writes you up
for sleeping on the job.
You lose a buck in the change machine
twenty at lunch poker.

Your kid's suspended from school.
Drugs, and your wife Loretta
blames you for ignoring him.

In the locker room, changing into
street clothes, you decide
to erase.

▼

After downing a few
at Bruno's Bar, you think
about calling home, but
your hands won't hold anything
smaller than a shot glass
so you keep throwing dollars
at Rachelle behind the bar.
She keeps the change.

Tomorrow with a fat head
of guilt and fuzzy pain
won't be any better.
You read every joke
on the bar napkin
without a smile.
No fun you write
in a puddle of beer.

You know what's next:
a cup of coffee, the quiet

ride home. You have your choice
of stories, all beginning with
mistake.

Rachelle kids you:
Diggin' your grave tonight,
eh Digger?
You open your eyes:
Another inch or two.

DIGGER'S MELTED ICE

Loretta takes the kids
to her sister's: *till you
calm down.*

Calm now, you cry softly
into fists, ice melted
in your glass. A few things
broken litter the house.

You brought Eddie home
for a nightcap. 3 A.M.
She kicked his butt
out the door. Started in about your drinking
again, about counseling. *I've talked
to Father Steve,* she said. She tilted
your bottle toward the sink. Your hand
held her wrist till she let go.

You fill your flask for work.
Last year, you switched from fifths
to half gallons. *Economical.*
You turn on the TV: a movie
about a reporter who'll do anything
to get his story. *Goddamn priest.*

Tomorrow you'll call Loretta.
Apologize. Maybe she'll be home already
like other times.

You think about your machine,
how you push two buttons and the press

comes down. Always the same,
so simple you can disappear.

Your son asked you once
why you drink so much.
Part of my job, you said.

DIGGER, DEEP SNOW

A sudden day off.
You invite neighbors over
to shoot pool in the basement
to fill the deep silence. You drink
fast to get inspiration to talk
about something besides snow.

After a few drinks, Tony rips
the felt with his cue
when Gus kids him about his fat wife.
Herb and Brad wrestle, breaking
glass, falling into washtubs.
The fridge empties. Ed leaves
to pick up a couple more bottles.
Hard stuff, he winks.

Outside, drifts pile above
the basement windows. Inside
Willie and Frank argue about jobs:
How can a guy get ten bucks an hour
for sweeping floors?
Who's gonna do it for less?
You down your drink,
start to mix another:
Stronger? Weaker?
You shake your watch,
hold it to your ear.

DIGGER'S TRIP

You pull into a rest stop,
tired of rain, the roadside billboards blaring
how many miles to the next mystery spot
or mystery hole, a place where gravity's
all messed up and people pay
to see upside-down rooms, balls rolling uphill.
Your daughters want to stop and see one.
It wouldn't be a mystery anymore,
you tell them. *We'll see
alligators in Florida.*
They crinkle up their faces.

You wait, drumming
to an oldies station, wipers
waving in time. Your daughters
run back to the car while you rock
your head like a windshield wiper,
tongue lolling back and forth.
For a second, Loretta's mouth
hangs open like your own
and you want to press yours
against hers
to see if the tongues
will talk again,
talk like that again.

Sunburned, you wear your Tiger's hat
to the beach, Stroh's towel
draped over your shoulders.
Your wife and daughters wear T-shirts:
Sterling Plant, Home of the Axle.

You want everyone to know:
a Detroit family—we do real work.

When you leave the beach
for the last time
an old man under an umbrella
grabs your arm as you pass:
I worked at Chevy thirty-five years
then retired down here.
Is this the life, or what?
He holds on till you nod.

That night
at a motel in Georgia
the sand in your shorts
is that old man.

▼

In Ohio a tire blows.
Your spare's flat too.

Loretta and the kids wait
while you roll the spare back
toward the last exit.
Trucks blow you to the edge
of the shoulder. You feel like
a doll somebody's playing with.

The gas station charges you twenty.
Rip off, you spit, pushing the tire
back to your car. *Some doll,*
you think, and roll right past the car

and down the road. In twenty-four hours
you'll be back on the job.
You hear Loretta call your name
but you keep on going.

DIGGER PLAYS HARDBALL

At the family reunion
you play first base
because you're biggest
bat clean-up
because you're biggest.

When you hit one
over all their heads
first time up
and trot around the bases
you feel that ball inside you
going places.

You pop-up
the rest of the game.

▼

You made your son cry
the only time you played catch together.

At a Little League game
another father mocks your son
after a bad throw.
That's my son shuts him up.
He quits the team after half a season.
That's okay, you tell him,
get a paper route.

DIGGER, POWER, SPEED

*Toys. Wimpmobiles. That's what
we're making now.* Sitting on the stoop
with your brother the engineer
who just bought an Escort,
you shake your head, *My own brother,
going small-time.* He smiles,
quotes mileage and dollars.
But how's it drive?

You jerk the lever—
Don't this seat move back any?
Heading up a slight rise
you punch the gas. It hesitates,
struggles, catches. Your brother shrugs.
I'll never drive less than eight,
you tell him, *this little fourbanger, man,
they'd've laughed you off the street
for driving one of these suckers
back in '66.*

Ain't '66 no more, bro, he says
*and these little cars
are saving your job.*

Yeah, yeah, yeah. You know
he's got you, they've all got you,
and there's not enough room,
not anywhere.

▼

Motor City Dragway, Sunday afternoon, August.
You sit in the splintered grandstands with Loretta
watching six seconds of noise and speed and flames.
Only things you do fast now are eat and drink.
You wipe the sweat from the brim of your hat,
place it back over your bald spot. *Speed.*
Fast enough to get away.

Loretta leans her head against your arm, rubs
a hand across your sweaty back. You look at her:
There's something sexy about all this,
you know. She laughs, pats your arm, *Maybe.*

You drive home on a thin, straight road
into the growing night. She slides close
at a red light and kisses you ear.
Vroom vroom, you say, *vroom, vroom.*

DIGGER GOES TO CHURCH

Christmas Eve you stumble
into the packed midnight mass.
An usher finds a seat for your wife.
You lean back against the wall.

You try to recognize faces
or find women to stare at
while the priest drones on.
You want a smoke. You spot your son
standing on the other side.

In the middle of mass
one of his friends
recites prayers out loud
at the wrong times. He falls
to the tile yelling out
the Our Father. Four ushers
rush up the aisle, drag him out.

Minutes later he's back in
and headed toward the altar.
Ushers rush to block his way.
The priest drones on.

The kid's shouting
This is bullshit, this is all
bullshit! Ushers grab him.
That's what church is all about—
holding people back. You think about that
while he fights the ushers, kicks
and flails as they drag him out.

Just as the priest starts again
the kid kicks out a window.

The priest spreads his arms
in a holy gesture. You want
to punch his fat gut.

Holding people back—you watch
your son follow them out the door.
He's on drugs, you think
and my son too, all messed up.

You clench your fists and step
out the door as mass is ending
as the priest wishes everyone
a Merry Christmas: *my ass.*

DIGGER PAYS OFF THE MORTGAGE

You write the final check,
lick the final stamp.
Loretta smiles,
hands on your shoulders.

That's that.
You set the envelope aside
and pull her to your lap.
Kiss her on the cheek.

*Think of all the extra money
we'll have each month,* she says.
*How are we going to spend it?
College for the kids, maybe.
Maybe we can get a place up north?*

Give us bigger allowances, your daughter
says from the doorway. *Bigger allowances?
I was getting ready to cut you off—
time for you to get a job.*

No way. She's fifteen. She makes a face,
stomps away. Loretta gets up.
Dishes, she says, pecking you hard
on the forehead.

You watch TV, your usual shows, then the news.
Everyone's in bed. You turn out the lamp
by your chair and look out the front window
at the spot on your lawn
where you planted three trees,
where they all died.

DIGGER TAKES HIS DOG FOR A WALK

After work you change
into shorts and sneakers, rattle
the leash to bring Clint running.
The doctor recommended
exercise. *Hey, I do*
physical work, you argued.
He sunk a finger into your belly.
Clint yanks at the leash.
You yank back, choking him.

He pulls you along, pissing
on every tree. *Might get you*
fixed, you don't settle down some.
When he was a puppy, you cupped
his soft balls in your hand.

You notice a light on at Stan's—
he works afternoons too. You hit
the bars with him after work.
Years ago.

Other dogs howl against fences.
You're a lucky dog, you laugh out loud.
He snorts into the clear night, buries
his nose in tall grass. You want
to get down on all fours and join him.

▼

Lights on at Gemanski's on the corner,
music blasting out a screen door. *Old man*
would've kicked ass for that. Bud dead
five years now: heart.

Trash cans line the street, brimming
with decay. You pull the dog away.
A pickup creeps by, busted chair, TV, in back.

Casalli's dark window: Steve on chemo, fading
into a dirty rag. Then Roy's old place, him shot
by his son. You hurry toward the next streetlight.

Then Johnsons'. Years ago you fought
because your kids fought. Over a broken bat.
You lost two days' work. His kid was right.

At the last corner, Turner's picker bushes
keep you from cutting across. His house, yard,
biggest on the block. He owns a shop, nonunion.
You never liked his slick hair
and glad hand. You don't know why he still
lives here, except to lord his money
over those with less.

Just a sliver of moon tonight.
The corner streetlight glows
with a warmth you wish was inside you.

You pull Clint to a halt
on Turner's perfect lawn: *C'mon boy,*
you whisper, *how about a nice crap?*
He sniffs around a tree. *Go. Go.*
And he goes.

DIGGER'S TERRITORY

Some would say
there's not much to
a life lived on your street.
They might say you're dumb
you watch too much TV
you drink too much
fart and belch and laugh too loud
dress funny, eat too many burgers.

But tonight after work
after you wash your hands
eat a good meal
wrestle with the dog a little
after you grab a beer
and sit with your family
on your porch sharing a laugh
with a couple neighbors
while the sun sets behind
the bowling alley, after a man parks
his car carefully behind
your Impala up on blocks
and walks stiff up your driveway
in his suit and briefcase and perfect hair
and holds out a soft hand,
you all smile at each other
because no matter what he knows
you're going to teach him
a few things.

4

Trouble at the Drive-In

On the other end

of the block
a kid with my last name
shoots his sister.
She was bugging me,
he tells the cops.

That night our phone rings
shrill with discretion.
We take it off the hook.

The girl will live.
I walk by their house.
Three girls jump rope next door.
Wasn't me I tell them.
They stop singing.

Years ago, I soaked in the bitter
night oil, ready to explode
with any random spark. Certain moments—
I could make a list.

Home from work, my sister
drinks a Coke, watches a soap.
She smiles at me: *Don't shoot.*
I take her head in my hands
like a piece of ripe fruit,
like the opposite of gun.

JOY RIDE

Laid off, my brother drove to Texas
with his wife, two kids, and a tent.
Came back burned, a mortgage
waiting to kick his ass.
Uncle Les got him a job driving trucks
north to Saginaw for a chain
of nonunion restaurants,
6:30 to 6:30, no overtime pay,
no pension. He watches his kids
on his day off while his wife works.

Today after calling in sick
he talks of quitting. Tunes up his car
in the street, an old Ford held together
with duct tape and mirrors,
then takes off on this first fine
April day down I-75 past the sign
announcing the number of new cars built,
past the brewery, the stadium, then south
into flatness to Monroe, home of La-Z-Boy
chairs, and down across the Ohio line
to drink in the first bar he can find
until he feels a fuzziness in his head
he can almost mistake for possibility.

You know the rest: he sobered up.
He drove home.

POSING

Broke and out of work
Rick read the ads each day
sitting at our scarred wooden table
playing games with dice,
rattle and *roll.*

None of us in our thin brown house
made much—Ellen, a chambermaid
at Sleep Cheap, Bev, waitress
at Big Boy's, me, night janitor
at the bank.

We kicked in $5 a week for food
turned the thermostat to the edge
each winter night. After two months
we hid his dice.

The day he took the job posing
for an art class at the college,
he yanked at his beard
and did not hum or pace.

We smoked homegrown,
sweat staining his one good shirt,
before he headed down to strip and stand
with his hair and skin and sadness.

▼

Back home: *they asked me to leave*
someone I know was there
the teacher was a jerk
they couldn't pay me enough. . . .

Then, finally, weeping
I couldn't hold still.
I said "Hey, if I had a job
I could hold still."

And those of us with jobs
were still until the moment passed,
then someone rose
and got out the dice.

BROKE

I-75 near Livernois
my '68 Satellite dropped
its drive shaft.
I guzzled my beer
though I wanted to puke
thinking about the money
I didn't have.

I walked to a gas station
where a man with a gun
in his back pocket
got me a tow truck.

I gave the driver
one of my beers.
His chapped hands bled.
In the cold cab
smelling of french fries
and oil, I tried to joke
but he wasn't joking.
Halfway home I calculated
the cost of the tow
plus the drive shaft
was worth more than the car.

He dropped it in the street,
yellow lights circling over bricks.
Some people looking out
I could see. Despite the beer
he overcharged me.
Orange lights racing
caution through my gut,
my wallet entirely too thin.

He threatened to take the car
back to the garage till I paid
the rest. I waited him out.
We both knew the car
wasn't worth shit.
I had two beers left
and I gave him one.

After he drove away
I sat on the curb
pulling pieces of rust
out of the door. Tomorrow
I'd make the rounds of junkyards
looking for a drive shaft
with my sincerity and bad check.

That week I'd applied for jobs
as a janitor, busboy, ice-cream man.
I was hoping for the ice-cream job—
a little joy behind the wheel
a little white truck
bells ringing through clean suburbs.

I made a little tower of rust
on the manhole cover.
Everything seemed that fragile.
Lying in wet snow, I'd clamped
a tin can over my broken exhaust pipe
to hold it together. A bean can.

Sucking on the tailpipe
taking a deep sleep:
that rusty thought gnawed me

while I sat next to the car
going no place.

I'd like to play it down,
that melodramatic night.
It's like when you see the flashers
and think it's the cops or an ambulance
but it's only a tow truck
hauling away another junker.

A few months later I got a decent job
but drove that old car longer than I had to,
held onto it like a nubby candle,
afraid getting rid of it
would jinx my luck. I had to lie
a little to get the job
but like the bean can
it was just another stretch.

I got a hundred for it
because it started and ran.
Sold it to a man who knew
all about tin cans.
We shook hands in the street.
I gave him the block of wood
I used to hold the heater vent open,
a little something solid, a little gift.

1977

Summer. Hot tar smell cramped our days,
dark oil smell crippled our nights
and we drank and smoked till our brains were mush.
And the weeks ran together, the seven-day weeks:
each night we punched out, sped off
to spill our maps, squinting in dim bars
sticky bars, bars of cement and piss
and twisted dollar bills. We had two weeks coming
and we had to make them count.
Two weeks. California.

We bought speed for the drive, and enough pot
for six months. We planned tattoos and Vegas sins.
We tuned up Artie's old Chevy, we punched in
    and out,
we blurred our syllables. We would save
our good clear voices.

August at last. We slammed our doors,
drove out of Detroit, blaring Ryder, Seger, Aretha.
We pounded our fists on the cracked dashboard,
pounded our chips and cold beer.

We drove through corn and wheat
and whatever else grows in Iowa
only to find Nebraska. We spun out
near the Colorado line. We passed out
in a rest stop lot—it was as far
as we'd ever been.

Speed jangled us into mountains
where we stopped to breathe.

The feeling started to come back
into my numb hand.

A cop wearing a softball uniform
pulled us over in Utah. *It's the boss,*
I told Artie, *he's followed us out here.*
Boss everywhere, Artie said, hiding the dope.

I pushed back my greasy hair and smiled.
He let us go because we were lost
cases. *Two weeks,* I told him, *we have two weeks.*
He knew what two weeks meant.
Softball wasn't enough, I could tell.
He looked at me, then at Artie. *You boys*
need a rest, he said, *not this.*

But it was Utah, so we sped to Vegas
where we dropped our change into slot machines
and watched high rollers lose enough in one hand
to cover our whole trip.

At the California border we did our factory howls,
cracked open beers, and kept on.
We wore union T-shirts over our pale skins.
We dripped the pure sweat of simple heat
and cooked till we burned under Malibu mansions.

We stared at topless women. Stoned
in our old chlorine-bleached suits
we grabbed our fistfuls of sand.
California. What did we expect?

▼

What did we expect?
                    I cannot tell you
even now. Tonight, Artie sits
at his father's table. His table now.
His careful hands sort the smudged photos
like old baseball cards, and we talk
about the trip, the wild times, dreaming up
better stories, translating the photos
like revisionist historians, till Artie falls
silent into his beer, his belly hanging
down, navel exposed, the dark hole getting deeper.
1977, he says, like that was the end of something.

After the layoffs, I left town to find work.
Two weeks. He doesn't even get that now,
fry cook at an all-night place.

Our bottles sweat in August heat.
Outside, bushes and weeds scratch the air
and fences peel from their posts like dead skin.
He shares this place with whoever he can get
to move in. Nobody just now. Next door
a German shepherd snarls and crashes against
     the fence.

He never mentions the long tired drive home,
     how we stopped
speaking in Nebraska because the state would
     never end
and we wanted so bad to be home and we wanted
     so bad

not to be home, to have no clock pasted on our
    dashboard,
no boss in the rearview mirror. *What are we doing,*
he'd said, *arguing like this? It's not us.*

I never thought Artie was very bright
but that seemed so smart and obvious.
It was like my father explaining
sex, so simple it scared me
and I did not want to believe.

1977. The year we had the energy to try.
The place on our maps marked with a star,
the capital city of our lives where we learned
about borders. Maybe it was like magnetic fields—
sucked back to our jobs, we talked big at lunch,
suddenly demagnetized, wondering
what we were doing back. It was the first check.
It was every check. And when we fought
it was because we were alike and repelled each other.

Let me pitch that old simple metaphor. It's about
    bosses
setting us against each other, getting us to fight
for scraps of time and money. It's *not* us.

I get up to leave, but he wants to make me breakfast.
He wants to show me how he can break eggs
with one hand. I sit back down, fumbling
with my keys, nowhere to drive to.

STILL LIVES: BENITAU STREET

St. Rose stands boarded against faithful
criminals. Across the street in cracked
blacktop two basketball rims hang, bent
vertical into glasses, a twisted
vision of vacant lots stretching into fields
with each burning, each demolition.

On the corner, rubble sits piled
like a funeral pyre,
a child's shoe on top. Even dust
does not rise from this stillness.

Abandoned gas stations stare
at each other from their corners.
A bathroom door, *Men,* lies
flat on the ground.

A man sits on a porch,
eyes closed, chin against chest.
The man in the house behind him
leans on a baseball bat, face flattened
against screen.

A phone rings over this rubble.
It could be for anyone.
A phone rings. It rings
and rings.

STILL LIVES: SWEAT

The old woman pleads with her son
to leave a neighbor alone—
a fight over a ten-speed.
She dies from a hole in her gut.

The off-speed ice-cream music
twists itself into the rhythm of a siren.
Words barely dent this ambulance air.
Police stand under a street sign
where nothing points in the right direction.

The son's eyes, his hands twisting in cuffs,
sign the snake that swallows our lives.
The eyes of the police are scooped out
by tiny spoons, the repeated scenes.

The neighbor hugs what lies
between his arms: *I don't got no
bike.* Sweat drips down foreheads,
under arms, nothing like tears.
Kids on bikes ride laughing in circles.

The ambulance takes the mother.
The police take the son.
The neighbor follows the tracks
down his arm: *I don't got no, I can't
get no.* Maybe there's a little more room
on our small porches of summer sweat.
Maybe a little less.

ONE OF THOSE THINGS

He bought the gun out of a friend's trunk
for his wife while he was on the road.

She kept it in a paper bag
in her underwear drawer.

He gave a stag party
for a mechanic at the garage.

Late, everybody drunk, playing cards.
He lost a few, needed to touch his roll.

Couldn't find it. Who'd been there?
One guy left early. Nobody really knew him.

He took the gun, drove to the house
where the guy denied everything, got shot anyway.

In the morning he picked up
his wife and kids at her mother's.

She handed him the money—
hope you didn't need it.

They arrested him at work.
Eight years in jail.

He's just an ordinary guy. A guy
who'll help you move, fix your TV.

He grew up in the neighborhood, no trouble
to anyone. Played first base on my team.

TROUBLE AT THE DRIVE-IN

The sky is gray and it will be
raining soon and we're waiting in line
for the drive-in, the one on Eight Mile,
the border between Detroit and Warren and the
     anger
is stewing just like always, every day
guns pointed at our own dumb heads, every day
somebody else dumb enough to pull the trigger
because we're mad, mad and sick and dumb
and we're gonna get ourselves a little piece of
     something
even if it means taking it away from someone else
who don't have much, or else we're sick and tired
of everybody taking, so we're gonna
protect ourselves, by god, though god
don't seem to help much here—he's getting ripped
off too—and we all want to have our say
one way or another, so there's a lot of guns
in a lot of hands, yes, I'm thinking all this here
as it starts to pour, fucking rain like crazy,
and I say *fuck* to let you know I mean
business, just like I carry a gun,
so it's fucking raining and if you don't like it
then fucking get lost because I'm still going
to the movies—a Clint triple-header—
Fistful, A Few Dollars More, and *Good/Bad/Ugly,*
and all these good, bad, ugly people are leaning
on their horns and some asshole cuts his car into
     the line
up front and this big fat guy gets out of his car
     and runs
up to that car and he's screaming *fuck you* so

he means business, and he's pounding on the windows
yanking on the door, and he's getting soaked, but
he don't give a fuck, he is me and he is you,
and the guy in the car is me and you
and we're all kicking each other's asses
while the bosses are safe and dry
in Grosse Pointe or West Bloomfield or wherever
the fuck they live, laughing at *The New Yorker* cartoons
and thinking Woody fucking Allen is a genius, let me
tell you, Clint ain't no genius, but I understand
his movies, and I understand what's going on
up ahead, and I'm hearing sirens, and me and you,
we're in this together, buddy, just a couple dummies
like those two up there, and nobody's letting us in
and nobody's getting out, and it's only a matter of
     time
till somebody pulls a gun.

HOW MUCH LIGHT

Tony Valducci floods his yard
with light after Marge Chomski next door
gets mugged on her stoop.

Cops found Kenny Flynn last month
sitting at the wheel
bullet in his neck
outside a downtown motel.
In the wrong neighborhood,
everybody said.

Yet a cop tells Mrs. Chomski,
you don't live in the best neighborhood
you know.

I always thought this was
the best neighborhood:
—Tim Pilkowski after cutting his grass,
mopping sweat, chewing his cigar.
—Bradley Jones explaining
about radiators and hoses, sliding out
from under his car, breaking into a hymn.
—Edie Lacy skating down frozen streets
one tough winter, all of us suddenly graceful.

Maybe it's okay to get sentimental:
there's a run on dead bolts
at the hardware store, and porches speak
of broken lawn chairs, empty butt pots.
Gossip's the latest crime, the latest
home for sale.

Neighbors stand, hands in pockets
in Valducci's drive, admiring his lights,
talking about guns.

What's happening here I don't understand.
It's like my fight with Jed Stark in 4th grade.
We faced off and he started punching.
We'd always wrestled before.
I said *no punching*
but he kept punching
I said *no punching*
but he wouldn't stop.

Jim Daniels was born in 1956 in Detroit. His first book, *Places/Everyone,* was selected by C. K. Williams as the winner of the 1985 Brittingham Prize for Poetry. *Punching Out,* his second collection, is a book-length sequence of poems about a young autoworker who comes of age in the Motor City. Daniels is also author of the screenplay for *No Pets,* a 1993 film by director Tony Buba. Daniels lives in Pittsburgh, where he teaches writing at Carnegie Mellon University.

PITT POETRY SERIES

Ed Ochester, General Editor